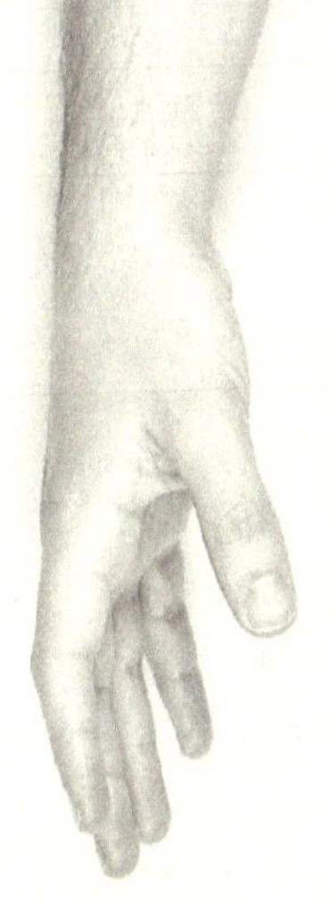

# Twin Flame Separation PAIN

## TIPS FOR HEALING AND RECOVERY

### SILVIA MOON

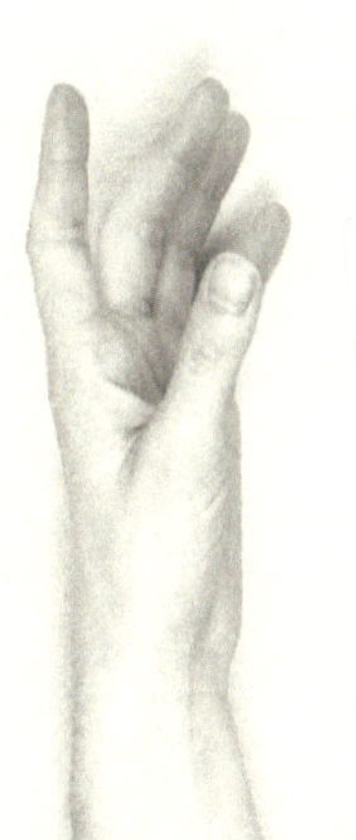

# Twin Flame Separation Pain

**Silvia Moon**

*I dedicate this book to you my dear Twin Flame
going through the separation phase*

# REVELATIONS

I now understand the meaning of the Twin Flame mirror effect. The Twin Flame simultaneously triggers within you your deepest desires and greatest fears.

I had severe early childhood trauma that pushed me to create intense coping mechanisms. I was considered mature for my age but my innocence was taken away at an early age. I lived in survival mode from thereon.

I have always been a loner; I know how to keep myself as my company. I thrive in solitude -- meditation comes easily to me. My childhood was a lonely one. I am your true definition of abandonment. I did not have a warm nest to call home as most children have.

Most of the time, I had to fend for myself; find food and shelter. My daily motivation was finding food and a warm place to crash at the end of the day. I was always in survival mode.

My ability to be vulnerable around him empowered me to travel back within myself to face the darkest corners of my Soul.

It never dawned on me that making meaningful connections was important. I never felt that I needed to feel loved -- I thought that it was not that important.

When I became an adult, I had relocated to a community where connections, relationships, and family were more important than living in survival mode. I knew right away that I did not belong. A sense of feeling loved and connected to the community is a natural human condition. It was very alien to me.

I had to submit to my new life situation. I tried my best to fit in the only way I knew how. I tried to be invisible. I suppressed myself; I always kept to myself, I downplayed anything about me that would make me stand out. I also suppressed my beauty both inside and outside.

When I became independent and moved away, I struggled to find myself; I felt stuck within myself in the world of many. I also put my emotional guard down and grew the strength to start dating. I thought I had fallen in love and also got married. I still struggled with myself every day. I had to look in the mirror and acknowledge myself; I could see that there were parts of myself that I was hiding from.

When I acknowledged my fears further, I knew that my inner child was suffering. I had been occupied by the everyday human condition that I completely ignored myself. I needed to find myself. For me to find my authenticity, I had to dig deeper within to heal. I knew that I would never find happiness in the material world if my inner child was unhappy.

Apart from having an abandoned inner child, I also felt disconnected from the world and everyone around me. Even though I was in relationships with other people, I still felt like something was missing.

I never felt like I fit it. To most people I seemed happy; I had an okay marriage, my business was thriving, and I was also traveling the world. I went to fancy places and met reputable high society individuals -- I felt uncomfortable and out of place most of the time.

When I met my Twin Flame, I felt an uncanny familiarity with him mostly because I could feel his pain as much as I felt mine. I did not know his life story then but I had an imminent knowing that he had been through similar childhood circumstances even though we grew up on different continents. Easy Surrender Tips For Beginners.

When I looked into his eyes the first time, he saw me as much as I saw him. Instead of feeling scared of someone for the first time seeing me for who I am, I smiled. I relaxed. I felt acknowledged and accepted. From thereon, I shared my deepest secrets with him. I told him that I was hurting.

My Twin Flame told me about his childhood as well. He said that he always felt abandoned since he is the middle child of 6 siblings. He says that he was always the "forgotten" one.

Since I knew of him 5 years before our meeting, mutual friends always talked about how he was looking for a home. He had searched the whole world looking for where to belong. When we finally met, we looked knew right away that we are each other's home. I could see how peaceful he was around me. He let his inner child come out when he is around me. I saw and felt how happy I made him feel.

My ability to be vulnerable around him empowered me to travel back within myself to face the darkest corners of my Soul. I found the courage to face and hug my inner child. I embraced every part of me. I freed myself from all sorts of fears and insecurity. I allowed myself to feel loved through Self-love.

I broke down all the walls that I had built against love. I allowed myself to feel loved unconditionally.

When we physically separated, I knew that he was my mirror staring back at me showing me the steps that I needed to heal myself. Our encounter then triggered me into an accelerated Spiritual Awakening process. Confronting my issues was easy but submitting to the changes was challenging.

For any healing to happen, I had to adapt to new routines and drop the previous old routines that I previously followed. I had to unlearn the old habits that did not serve me any good. I changed my sleeping patterns to have more time to rest. I changed my friends and life situation in alignment with my authentic self.

Well, you just hit the nail on the head. I am with you on this. We should preach this! Thank you for being honest. When my Twin Flame also avoided me, I said to him; "Thank you for avoiding me. If you hadn't done it, I would never realize how insecure I am." I was not kidding. I love him so much that his absence made me go back into myself to fix whatever was not working. As long as you are happy and safe within yourself, everything will be alright. I appreciate you for this!

I did not know that I was capable of becoming the person I am today; Brave, independent, content, simple, happy, and always forgiving.

My biggest lesson so far is learning to forgive myself. I now realize that I gave myself more shit than most people did. I tortured myself with negative thinking. My insecurities led me to people and places that I now see as bad influences. Every day when I see 11:11, I say a thankful prayer to God or the Universe for opening my eyes. For empowering to feel happy. For bringing true love to me. For my Twin Flame. Every day I am thankful!

I feel like I just started living 3 years ago when I was triggered into a Spiritual Awakening by the encounter. I was raised catholic but I did not believe I was a Spiritual person.

I was conditioned to be so many things throughout life and unfortunately, I must admit that my life on this earth has been more of suffering than what people fantasize it to be like. I struggled to find my place; no one knows what they are doing and the sad thing is that we have mastered the art of lying about our life situations. The human condition is all about looking perfect and being good. For me, if it was not for the Twin Flame Awakening, I would still feel lost and keep.

# The first meeting

*"What you seek is seeking you."*

Focus on preparing yourself for your Twin Flame; everyone out there has a Twin Flame including you!

If the timing is not right, you cannot force the connection. I knew of my Twin Flame for over 5 years before I met him. I was married to his friend. They have been friends for 25 years.

I heard stories about him before I met him — I knew that he wasn't my cup of tea.

A year before we met, I skipped lunch with him that was organized by mutual friends. He was in a committed relationship then. He wanted to meet me — his friend's wife.

We never had the chance to physically meet. I had spoken on the phone with him and I didn't feel anything special until that unexpected day!

He made an impulsive decision to come to visit us — when I saw him, I kept wondering to myself where I had met him before — the uncanny familiarity. It felt like we knew of each other in another lifetime and we were just reconnecting.

What triggered the Awakening was the eye contact; we had been talking all day since his arrival and somehow our eyes locked over dinner. He sat across from me.

We both couldn't look away — we SAW each other. We both smiled. Ever since then, it has been a roller coaster of energetic merging.

It feels like he downloaded his energy into mine. I felt him with me everywhere I went. It overwhelmed me because our connection had nothing to do with sexual relations or romance.

I felt like I had met a guardian, a father, mother, brother, best friend, confidant, etc. I knew that I had found a home.

When I met my Twin Flame, he was single and I was married. The situation was very complicated for sure because we both did not know what was going on. We felt the connection but I was not tempted to cheat on my husband.

The connection and us finding each other was more fulfilling than just the physical sexual intimacy. It was like my guardian had finally arrived; my home. I had been in relationships before I met my Twin Flame and I thought I knew what love was until I met.

I do not know if you agree with me but I believe that you cannot choose the situation in which you find each other.

Despite this, I also believe that it does not justify cheating, or hurting others in the process of changing our lives in hope of a reunion.

Secondly, just because we have to go through painful experiences to grow and clear our energy, it does not mean that we should inflict pain on our divine partners with narcissism and those around us.

I believe that Twin Flame love brings peace. It heals you, your Twin Flame, and those around you. Twin Flame love brings blessings.

Every day after you meet a Twin Flame is magical and way much better than before whether you are going through difficult times or not. The only pain you feel is all that was lodged within you. Your Twin Flame exposes all your core wounding.

Your Twin Flame is not SUPPOSED to bring you pain. You feel blissful feeling connected to him or her. You feel happy feeling their energy while you sleep. You feel your fear oozing out of you. You feel light beaming out of you. You feel blessed to be a Twin Flame.

# The Connection does not fade

*"Absence makes the heart grow fonder."*

When we are together, the connection is effortless. I always feel a harmonious balance between our energies— it is a heavenly feeling.

The connection always feels natural; like is meant to be. I always feel like the universe is working towards helping us love each other more.

When I am with my Twin Flame; it is total Oneness — One heart, one mind, and a happy Soul.

We operate as a Single Energetic Unit. When we are apart — the connection intensifies.

But, you learn to live with the absence of your Twin Flame because you feel comforted by the connection. You believe that no matter where he or she is in the world, they feel you too. When you focus on your life — you finally find inner peace.

# Separation Pain

I did not know what to do with myself three years ago when we separated. I went through manic depression for over 6 months.

Without him in my life, I felt a void within that nothing could fill no matter what I tried. I wanted the earth to swallow me whole. When he left, I was surprised that half of me was missing — I did not know about Twin Flames then. I had no idea that I was awakening to the Twin Flame connection.

The biggest side of my heart was the space that he left. I cried myself to sleep every night. I wailed on top of my voice while I was in the shower. I was always lovesick. I found it hard to leave my bed. I could not control the intensity of the shared energy.

Even though I felt sad and lonely without my Twin Flame, I had to function in the normal world. I had over 12 employees to manage at the same time; I was a CEO of a big company then.

I lost about 10 pounds of weight in 6 months. My friends could not understand my situation — I could not fully disclose the details because none of them had encountered a Twin Flame before. I also did not understand fully what was happening to him. I did not have the right words to express my feelings.

On top of all this mess, I was going through a divorce. When I met my Twin Flame, my life changed for the better; it first got worse though. Three things that perplexed me — the heart palpitations, ringing ears, and puking.

When the energetic share is too intense with my Twin Flame, the pressure is only released when I throw up. Heart palpitations happen when he is thinking of me. Ringing in the ears happens when there is an energetic shift in our shared frequency.

It is okay and normal to feel sad, lonely, lethargic, and physically ill. I have been through it all. There are moments when you will feel extremely happy and joyful.

Suddenly, you feel sad and helpless like nothing can save you from your pain. I call this the emotional rollercoaster.

I tried many things to help me stop feeling this way including trying to sever the bond — nothing worked. I tried drinking myself to sleep but it only made me feel worse about myself.

Even though you are advised to heal your pain, it is a process to find the light at the end of the tunnel. Sometimes you feel like you have made tremendous progress and other days feel like you are relapsing.

When I did emotional work, I felt stuck most of the days. I was in limbo most of the time and nothing would ease the pain of missing him. I would close myself in my bedroom when I was lovesick. I cried myself to sleep. I could not stop the heart pulling from him.

When I tried to surrender, I knew that I was forcing it because I was not ready to free myself from fear and pain. I would write to him very long letters to explain to him about my feelings and the experiences that I went through. I still was in denial of the Twin Flame phenomenon — I thought that the experiences were very complicated for me to go through. I was very intimidated by the nature of the Twin Flame process.

Even though he rarely responded, I felt understood by him. I also knew that my Twin Flame is the only person who would understand me. Most of my friends thought that I was going crazy or maybe obsessed with him. Others thought that it was a temporary love crush that would eventually fade over time. I can now testify to the fact that they were all wrong.

I finally found solace within the connection by accepting my Twin Flame through the heart space. I had to surrender and submit because there was no going back to my old self and life situation. All my friends whose attitude and energy did not align with my new Twin Flame energetic vibration had to go.

I told him about my situation and how I felt for him; I thought that he would understand — I made the situation awkward and he uncomfortable. We became estranged. He said; "It is best for everybody if we don't talk to each other". I knew what he meant because I was still married to his friend.

I became more depressed after our conversation. I thought that I had lost him forever.

I could still feel our connection even though we didn't talk.

I was very perplexed by his response because I knew that we both acknowledge that we have a special bond.

I missed how he looked into my eyes to tell me the truth of his soul. I missed how he respects me — he cares for me and always protects me.

I could not believe why everything felt like we are RIGHT for each other but the timing was wrong.

For me, the struggle was battling with all sorts of Fears. I blocked him because I was afraid of embracing the changes that he triggered within me and my life situation. My life turned upside down first. So much chaos swept through everything— I was not ready to change myself. I thought that blocking him would make all the chaos stop. The more resistance I put up against feeling the connection, the more I dig deeper into my pain.

Secondly, I was afraid of what people in my community would think of me if I abruptly dissolved my estranged marriage. I was afraid of being judged by my peers.

I was also afraid of separating my family and friends if I divorced my husband. That means I was separating others.

Lastly, I was afraid of the uncertainty that followed suit after the changes. I was not sure if I divorced and freed myself, my Twin Flame would still be there waiting.

I had nowhere else to go but within myself. I knew that I had abandonment issues to work on — plus I needed to find solutions to my life situation.

I did not think that I was strong enough to overcome my issues — I was frightened when I faced myself the first time; I felt very uncomfortable.

I tried blocking my Twin Flame and forget about what we found in each other; Nothing worked.

I went through an intense phase of energetic purging. The Spiritual Awakening process transformed me.

I rediscovered Self-love; I finally Surrendered and let my Twin Flame be.

Oh lord, what an experience!

All in all, allow yourself to feel the pain and then heal from it. It does not matter how fast you get here but just know that you are stronger than you think.

I tried to find suitors. I felt like the Universe was blocking me.

I felt trapped every time I tried to find someone. I knew deep within that I was running from myself and trying to hide behind other relationships and people only left me feeling isolated and lonely.

It felt like purgatory; there was no specific map to help me come out of my misery.

Only you know the truth of how you feel within. If you genuinely want to move on and date someone new, the Universe would let you.

You both suffer endless heartaches in quiet desperation. You live in purgatory forever until you confront the situation. The true Twin Flame nature is Union. You are already one — you have to break from the chains of the Human condition to realize wholeness.

# Runner Stress

We had just separated for a week. I thought that I was okay without him. I resisted thinking of him. I tried not to feel the connection. I forced myself to go about my daily routines like I did not feel the emotional chaos.

Deep down, I missed him so much. I experienced all kinds of emotional chaos. My mind and my heart were conflicted but my Soul was home when we met.

I was driving on the highway when I felt painful emotions flowing towards me that were not mine. It was my first time to experience his pain. It came in form of a ball of pain rolling around my heart area. His pain hurt me more than mine did. I suddenly broke down into tears and wailed in my car as I drove home.

When I got to the house, I did not want to talk to anyone. I closed myself in my bedroom until the next morning.

When I woke up, I felt worse than before. I was lovesick -- I could feel my heart area heating up with warm feelings of love. I was new to feeling the alien emotions that I felt powerless. I went into a mild anxiety attack. I was surprised that I could still feel the connection to him even though I tried my best to avoid him.

The inner resistance that I put up to resisting the connection manifested as physical illness. I struggled to breathe. My body felt weak as I got cold sweats. I was in denial.

When I finally recovered 30 minutes later, I started researching about my experiences. Luckily enough, this is when I learned about the Twin Flame experiences. When I learned about the nature of the process, I realized that perhaps I had met mine.

I continued to study myself and my experiences; I now believe that I truly found the only love of my life.

# Trauma Vs Upsets

I was born into a life of trauma. Every day that I lived, I was always in survival mode. Only the basic things mattered to me like food, shelter, clean water, etc. I did not care much about staying healthy, feeling loved, and or about my physical appearances.

That was a luxury to me. I did not choose to be born into that kind of lifestyle until I realized as a young adult that it was not normal.

Realizing and acknowledging that something is not good for you does not automatically change you and your life situation. There is a process that you go through to unlearn negative conditioning -- you break down the walls that you had previously built around yourself and your heart.

The process of changing, unlearning, and growing does not happen overnight. For me, it took years of self-rediscovery.

The moment I met my Twin Flame, I was in the phase of questioning my life as I knew it. I felt like there was something more to life than merely existing. I did not have a footing or a grounding within myself.

I questioned who I was because I did not feel like I had a foundation of my identity. I felt like I was just floating through life. I used to ask myself; "What is the meaning of my life?"


*Here is how I distinguish my Trauma from an upset:*

My Trauma was lodged within me from childhood. I inhibited past life abandonment issues. My inner child was struggling to be healed.

I learned that apart from my inner child struggling, I did not know myself. I had never had the opportunity to understand who I was. I was a stranger in my body.

When I met my Twin Flame, everything felt aligned; It was like a veil was finally lifted. I could see myself because he is another version of me in another body.

We compared notes about Spirituality, life, ourselves, and the human condition.

We taught each other love and life lessons. We also gave each other the map on how to heal -- we inspired each other to learn to love unconditionally starting with self-love.

When we physically separated, the side effects of my trauma took effect. I felt insecure.

I did not feel like I was worthy of his love. I felt incapable of loving him unconditionally since I had never felt it before. I had never been loved by anybody unconditionally. I also felt uncomfortable feelings of vulnerability; Twin Flame love disarmed me. I felt exposed to my Twin Flame. I was fearful of letting my guard down and get hurt.

Because of trauma from the past, I thought that I was unlovable. I had fears of exposing myself to my Twin Flame because I thought that he would eventually abandon me as most people did in my past life.

Instead of allowing myself to embrace unconditional love, I resisted the connection and blocked my Twin Flame out of my life.

*Lastly, this is what Core Upsets are from my experience:*

After I blocked my Twin Flame because of the issues arising from a wounded inner child, I was triggered into the release of my past pain. Past Pain is when I repressed negative feelings and emotions over time because I did not want to confront them.

Every time I was hurt or upset about something, I pretended that it did not bother me.

When I was triggered by the Twin Flame encounter to awaken to myself, I experienced a lot of emotional chaos.

I felt all sorts of negative feelings arising out of me -- I could not control the process. I blamed my Twin Flame for triggering the pain. I was angry, frustrated, and overwhelmed.

At this point, I wished that I had never met him.

# Running From Love

When you meet a Twin Flame, you have an imminent feeling that he or she is yours and you are theirs no matter what separates you. You see each other in a way that nobody else does. The more I ran from my Twin Flame, the more I was hit by the truth that soon or later, I will have to confront him and our uncomfortable situation.

I also partly blocked him because I was still married. All in all a Twin Flame is like a beautiful curse; you live inside each other and you cannot escape the beautiful love connection no matter what you do to deny how you feel. You are the missing piece of the puzzle to each other.

I have no desire to be with anyone. I cannot wait to be single forever if my Twin Flame does not work his issues out. I would rather be alone than be with him if he is still hurting. After a few years of celibacy, I tried to date again. I had no desire to intimately connect with anyone. I feel fulfilled and satisfied by the Spiritual nature of the connection. I feel at peace and free of fear. I feel more of a Spiritual being through a human condition. I feel blessed to know unconditional love, inner peace, and joy. I am grateful to the universe for all my blessings.

# Stalking the Chaser

Before beginning this discussion, you have to accept that you are capable of being both the runner and the chaser. You are your Twin Flame. You have both the divine feminine and masculine energy. When you understand that you are your Twin Flame, yous top judging him or her. You grow more empathy. You also find forgiveness for each other easily.

My Twin Flame and I have been chasing each other for over the past three years. I am at a phase where I only seek inner peace. I stopped stressing about what he is doing on the other continent. We both acknowledge the connection; I am content that when the timing is right, we shall see each other again.

## Religiously following your social media

When a Twin Flame is stalking you on social media, you always tell because you feel him or her lurking in the shadows. You realize that he or she will make incredible efforts to create a pseudo account to keep up with your status updates. Whenever you post something new, you realize that there is always that strange person who always likes your posts or also views your stories.

Your Twin Flame can also stalk your friends and family who regularly like your posts. The runner will do all they can just to have all the information about the divine lover even though he or she denies the love connection.

If you stop chasing him or her, you will realize that they will start chasing you so that you can be triggered into the running and chasing cycle.

### *Checking on you through friends*

I was surprised by a friend's visit yesterday. He is the one that my Twin Flame always sends to check on me all the time. He had no good reason to drop by and he insisted to talk to me. It was a very awkward situation because the was surprising.

You always know when a Twin Flame is trying to reconnect with you. You feel him or her pull you in with their energy. before his friend showed up at my door, I felt my Twin Flame all day. I meditated for over an hour and I embraced the connection with my heart space.

A while ago, my Twin Flame called home for over two hours talking about what is going on with his life. I wondered to myself; "If he is so happy wherever he is and he does not want to talk to me, why does he keep calling?" He calls my closet friend and he spills his guts. If you are a Twin Flame who is struggling with healing and Surrender, do not worry.

You will eventually overcome your fears and your pain. You reach a stage when you feel endless inner peace and harmony. You start to manifest success and abundance. You feel free of fear and insecurity. When you start beaming with unconditional love and light, you become a threat to those stuck in the negative patterns -- you rub them the wrong way.

I have also learned that when your heart starts radiating love, you feel it flowing towards your Twin Flame as well. You feel the magnetism of your love pulling you closer back to each other. You know deep within that your Twin Flame feels your vibrant energy and this is the reason why he or she feels compelled to return.

It is indeed true that when you heal, it boosts your shared energy with your Twin Flame because you operate as a single energetic unit. Your Twin Flame runner will start chasing you if he or she is not yet healed because your energy attracts them back to the Source.

The runner feels you as much as you feel him or her. You are one in essence.

*Do we have to always have to chase or run from our Twin Flames? My TF and I are apart. We reconnected after 10 years and began speaking almost every day. We know that we'll be together. We long for more but aren't in any way running or chasing.*

This is a great question. From my experience, running and chasing is only a phase when Twin Flames are learning to embrace their shared energy of oneness.

The Twin Flame experience triggers you into a Spiritual Awakening and if you are not used to the intense energetic share, you feel confused and frustrated that you block your Twin Flame temporarily.

But also, once your energy improves and grows, you feel the energetic harmony with your Twin Flame.

Once I learned to embrace the shared energy of oneness with my Twin Flame, I completely left him alone and we started to talk every once in a while.

I feel the maturity of my energy and I am more content with feeling the connection than obsessively chasing him to communicate with him.

I believe that once you start feeling the connection from the heart space, you relax and enjoy your bliss because it feels very authentic.

For me, the running and chasing phase taught me lessons that I needed to grow and advance further on the journey.

It was a trigger for the intense Spiritual Awakening phase and once I evolved into my authentic self, I felt happier than before and I started appreciating the blessings of the Twin Flame experience.

# Anger Issues

I first was angry at my Twin Flame for evoking the overwhelming feelings that I felt. I blamed him for triggering my pain. I said to him; "I love you but stay away from me!"

I blocked him — I disconnected his Instagram. I deleted his phone contacts. I also deactivated my social media. I knew that I was done with him. It did not stop the connection from flowing through.

I started drinking to quiet the mental conversations: I wanted the telepathic communication to stop. I wanted to stop thinking of him — I could not switch off my mind. If I was successful with stopping the incessant thoughts, I felt his energy merging with mine. I could communicate with him in my mind. Sometimes I could hear whispers of his voice.

I was perplexed by how intense the connection became every time I tried to disconnect from him.

I also tried to date other people at the beginning of our separation phase. I thought that it would make me forget him. I was very unsuccessful— the Universe kept reminding me of how empty I felt without my Twin Flame.

Running away and hiding from him made me feel like I was hiding from a certain aspect of myself.

Well, the further I ran from him, the more I felt isolated from myself and the world around me. I hid behind drinking and surrounding myself with as many people as I could but I still felt lonely.

I felt like I was attached to my Twin Flame with an invisible rubber band; I felt the connection eating at me.

I traveled to fancy places looking for my Twin Flame in many people's eyes but I could not find him.

When you meet a Twin Flame, and you acknowledge each other, you know for sure that you found Home.

*Easy or west, home is always best.*

*If it is real, a Twin Flame runner misses you as much as you miss him or her. You feel the authenticity of your connection within you.*

# Healing

It has been a healing journey for 3 years and every day only gets better. I learned to embrace myself; the good, the bad, and the ugly. You are a Spiritual being going through a human condition. Your true nature is endless inner peace and harmony.

Let yourself feel the pain, let it come to the surface, and then cleanse it out of your system. You will finally grow an emotional muscle to main the state of inner harmony and balance.

You have to fight for love. Twin Flame love is worth fighting for. If you truly believe that he is your Twin Flame, you know that nothing can replace how you feel for him. I advise fellow Twin Flames that if you keep persisting and persevering, you eventually have a breakthrough.

Once you embrace your experiences and accept the nature of your situation, you first go through the uncomfortable phases of growing, energy cleansing, and the darkest phase of Spiritual Awakening like the night of the soul. Once you overcome the obstacles within.

You gain a new perspective. You have a paradigm change. You start to understand that the Twin

Flame journey is full of blessings. You learn to unlock your gifts of Spiritual Awakening.

You gain enlightenment. You realize that a physical relationship with a Twin Flame is only icing and you are Cake. I have also learned that it is not enough to work towards a reunion.

You have to prepare yourself to be the kind of person you can be in a relationship. You are mirror images. It is very complicated for a married Twin Flame. I know that for sure because I was also married before.

Life is more challenging because you not only have to think of yourself but also your karmic partner, extended family, and friends.

It is overwhelming when you think of divorcing because you know that you will be not only from your Karmic partner but everybody involved.

# The married Twin Flame

It sucks when you are the married twin Flame. I know the feeling because I was one. Our situation was your reverse— I couldn't stay away from him yet we needed the space to understand what had just happened to us.

Everything happened so fast: we both didn't know about Twin Flames. We could speak to each other without saying a word.

Life sucks without the divine lover. It sucks when you are the married twin Flame. I know the feeling because I was one. Our situation was your reverse — I couldn't stay away from him yet we needed the space to understand what had just happened to us.

Everything happened so fast: we both didn't know about Twin Flames. We could speak to each other without saying a word.

# Signs of inner union

- You feel unceasing inner harmony; you sit in your power. You feel unhurried — you are in control of your feelings. You feel endless inner peace. You feel connected to the source of your being.

- You do not worry about your Twin Flame's behavior. You feel the connection within you. You know for sure that he or she feels the same way. After you feel complete union within, you feel eternally married to your Twin Flame. You relax and watch your life unfold as it was divinely planned.

- You feel no envy or jealousy in case your Twin Flame is dating someone else. You have no fear that the connection would fade. You instead pity whoever your Twin Flame is dating because you know that you have an eternal pact with him or her.

- You also understand that even though your Twin Flame chooses to move on and marry someone else, you have their Soul. You know for sure that as long as you both walk the earth, you will never be happy with anyone else but each other.

- You trust the divine to guide your journey. If you were trying to be the driver of your Twin Flame bus, you give up the keys to the Universe and trust that you will arrive at your destination happily.

# Communication trouble

English is my second language. He was fascinated by my traditions and culture. He tried to learn phrases and sentences so that he could communicate with me. We sometimes mixed English with my language and we came up with our unique code of communication.

We could crack jokes and laugh at ourselves all the time. When it comes to telepathic communication, you have a sacred space that only the language of the soul can be understood. You shift out of your human condition and ascend into your spiritual self that defies all the rules of communication.

Your heart space embraces the flow of communication between you and your twin flame while unconditional love flows unceasingly. When Souls whisper to each other, it is the intimacy that speaks. The love language. It is very complicated to understand with the human mind. You have to experience it first.

I tried severing the bond but it did not work. The more I put up an inner resistance to feeling the connection, the more I felt pain. Trying to disconnect from a Twin Flame is impossible.

Apart from feeling the connection all the time, I always think of my Twin Flame without consciously putting in any effort. I tried to hide behind meaningless relationships hoping that I would forget him. I was frustrated that I was not prepared to meet him -- Having him in my life meant that I had to change my life situation.

I was not prepared to change. I thought that I was okay with my life before. I was somewhat happy; at least it is what I thought then. I now understand that there is no way out of this Twin Flame situation. I had to submit to the new changes -- nothing was easy at all.

I had to change myself inside out. I had to unlearn the old habits that did not serve me any good so that I could evolve. I had to ACCEPT my Twin Flame and our situation. When I finally Surrendered to our connection, I texted him saying; I accept you.

For me, I went through the different stages of the Dark Night of the Soul and I felt like I was grieving my Soul.

Twin Flame grief is not a mental illness but rather a coping mechanism to the intense emotional chaos and separation anxiety that accompanies the Soul Shock that you experience when you physically separate from your Twin Flame. When you experience the Soul Shock as a Twin Flame, you go through the different phases of coping with the loss of the other part of your Soul who is your Twin Flame.

*Should you text your Twin Flame during physical separation?*

Communication between you and your Twin Flame can get estranged along your Twin Flame journey but you learn to accept it as time progresses because there is not much that you can do to make your Twin Flame more responsive to you.

The more you learn the dynamics of the relationship with your Twin Flame, you also accept that what you feel from within is more important than physical communication. Twin Flames have unique telepathic communication and energy is the language.

I believe that if you mean well, you are free to send a message to your Twin Flame.

Make your messages encouraging, heartwarming, and full of love. No matter what you do, your Twin Flame is always happy to hear from you especially if you are sending them love.

Be honest and always tell the truth of your heart because you are one with your Twin Flame. Your Twin Flame can channel your pain and desire so they know how you feel about them.

Twin Flame love is a mutual connection and no matter how much you tend to deny it, it is inescapable. There is no doubt how your Twin Flame feels about you because you feel it within you.

# Energetic Communication

I know exactly what you mean. If the Twin Flame phenomenon did not exist, I would assume that I am going crazy.

If you have been on the Twin Flame journey long enough, you know that you have a special kind of energetic communication that is unique to just you and your Twin Flame.

I surrendered and healed; I feel happy without his presence but I get hints of him within me. It is very complicated to explain.

When I try to not think of him, I feel his energy pulling at mine as if he gets alerted. The time when we became estranged, I was surprised that I could feel him especially when he is happy.

I energetically feel alerted when he is intimate with someone.

*There is no moving on from a Twin Flame, is there?*

# Astral Projection

When we astral project, I feel it occupy our sacred space. You let go of the human condition and instead be the Spiritual beings that we are.

Astral projection is mutual; both your higher selves must open to each other.

For me, astral projection is different from telepathic communication because I can send telepathic messages to him without knowing if his channel is open. Sometimes I do not get his feedback right away.

Sometimes I receive his messages without me being interactive during telepathy.

Astral projection is instant for us — I am always on the same wavelength with him.

Astral projection makes missing him bearable.

# Runner Denial

Sometimes you wonder if your Twin Flame will ever return to you. You wonder if the encounter was an illusion and sometimes you doubt your feelings because you wish to sever the connection and move on from the emotional stress of missing your Twin Flame.

You wonder if you were deluding yourself in the first place or maybe you were being obsessed because you get tired of waiting for your Twin Flame to acknowledge the special bond that you share if they are in denial.

Doubting your Twin Flame connection brings so much emotional desolation and you feel as though you are disconnected from within.

When you are in a doubtful mood about your Twin Flame connection, you feel like you are denying an essential part of yourself who is your Twin Flame. The void in your Soul keeps reminding you that you are incomplete without them.

# Anger Issues

After the denial Phase wore off, emotional pain started to emerge from within. All the past pain that I had accumulated from the past rose to the surface.

Meeting my Twin Flame exposed the broken parts within me that I needed to work on and the encounter and then separation triggered the emotional chaos.

Sometimes I blamed my Twin Flame for making me feel frustrated and one time I angrily told him to stay away from me.

I was also frustrated that we met at the wrong timing because I was married — I wished that if we met we were both single, things could have been much easier to handle.

The next day when I woke up after blocking my Twin Flame, I felt frustrated because I could still the connection. My heart was racing faster than normal and my thoughts kept racing towards him. I was frustrated because I wanted it all to stop.

By then, I did not know anything about Twin Flames.

# Emotional Compensation

I started to compromise with my feelings wondering if blocking him was a bad idea. I wished that I had not chosen to block him — I was full of regret and worry that my Twin Flame was gone for good. This is when I started to chase my Twin Flame asking for forgiveness for blocking him out of my life. My Twin Flame became unresponsive to me, and I became very exhausted from the chasing actions.

In this phase, I was wishing that life could have been different if perhaps I had not blocked him out of my life. I started to wonder if blocking him was a bad idea — I started regretting the actions that I used when I tried to chase him.

The guilt that I felt pushed me to try and chase him to apologize for the actions of trying to block him out of my life. I had no idea that all the pain that my Twin Flame had triggered were to be cleaned out of me, and I did not know that I was going through a Spiritual Awakening process then.When I chased him, I thought that he would be the answer to all my problems. I thought that if he forgave me, I would feel better and mend our relationship. I was wrong.

# Depression and anxiety

I rarely share about my experiences when I went through an alcohol addiction to numb the pain of missing my Twin Flame. I did not know then that I was going through Twin Flame experiences.

I was naive, I thought that separation would make the feelings of missing him dissipate. It only amplified the chaotic emotions. Every time I felt my Twin Flame pulling me into the connection through telepathy, I resisted it.

I drunk more alcohol to put myself to sleep. Alcohol also helped me to silence my thoughts.

I always think of my Twin Flame 24/7. During the time of my addiction, life became worse than before I met my Twin Flame. I went through so many changes that were out of my control.

I regretted meeting him. I was very frustrated that I still felt him even though I tried so many ways to forget him. Not long after that, I was hit by intense waves of the Spiritual Awakening process. I went into the phase of the night of the soul.

I started realizing that what I was experiencing was not of the norm; this is when I found out about Twin Flames. I still was using alcohol to numb my pain.

It took me a year to feel strong on my own to embrace the Twin Flame process; there was no way around my situation. I had to go through it. After I healed my pain, my body started getting over alcohol.

It naturally happened; Embracing the Twin Flame connection brought more inner peace to me than alcohol would. I completely got overusing alcohol to hide my pain. Thanks for this!

I hurt my Twin Flame; I asked him for forgiveness — I was scared and drunk too. I regret it every waking day.

I had no idea who Twin Flames are 3 years ago. After almost a month of getting to know each other completely — we stayed together — he left to go back to his continent.

I could not believe that life without him seemed like limbo. I did not know how to be happy without him.

I was shocked he lived inside me. I wrote a very angry letter to him saying: "I love you without expectations. I am overwhelmed by my feelings. I feel like a teenager.

I am very good at hiding — it is what I am going to do. I love you and I don't want you to love me back."

I re-read my letters to him every day. I know that I wanted to express my honest feelings but it all can out wrong. I pushed him away. I know I did.

I, later on, accepted the confusion Twin Flame journey and submitted to the overwhelming feelings.

I apologized to him but sometimes I think I pushed him too far.

I still feel him every day more intensely than at the beginning.

# THE DARK NIGHT OF THE SOUL

This was the initiation of the night of the soul — I was pushed into cycles of energy cleaning and I had to face the darkest corners of my soul.

This phase put me to my knees and tamed my ego. I finally submitted to rediscovering myself by learning to embrace every broken part of me. I had to hug and heal my inner child.

It is like I was grieving my soul. My mind could not understand what my heart was feeling, therefore, my thoughts and emotions were in chaos. I was sad, hopeless and on normal days, I was numb to my surroundings.

I lost a taste for food, almost everything tasted the same and I could not get myself to see beyond my pain. I could wake up in tears, restless, and sometimes I could just feel depressed moment to moment.

# SURRENDER

This phase put me to my knees and tamed my ego. I finally submitted to rediscovering myself by learning to embrace every broken part of me. I had to hug and heal my inner child. This is when I finally found healing. Healing empowered me to confront every aspect of my Twin Flame experiences and I finally found a breakthrough with my Twin Flame.

So how did I stop chasing him?

When I was new to the Twin Flame experience, somedays seemed like everything was aligning into the direction of a physical reunion with my Twin Flame and other days seemed like I will never see him again. I was infuriated because I felt like I was moving 3 steps forward and 4 steps back. During other days, I felt like I was relapsing continuously.

No matter how much advice I looked for to help me understand if I was going to see him soon, nothing seemed to satisfy me. I was very miserable and life was starting to seem hopeless. I tried to Surrender at first and it did not work because I was mechanically treating the experience. I expected him to return once I succumbed to Surrender. I was so frustrated because nothing worked but I naturally eased into it finally.



You can surrender but you cannot let go of your Twin Flame because nothing can sever the bond that you share. You are eternally bound together in the Soul.

Surrender does not mean that you keep waiting for your Twin Flame but rather, it is the process of learning to free yourself within so that you can find inner harmony and healing.

You naturally feel exhausted from stressing about your Twin Flame and all you want is to feel free of the emotional pain.

You know that you will always feel connected to your Twin Flame energetically but finding healing and happiness affects you as a person but the energetic cleansing and growth affect both of you because of the shared connection.

Accept that Twin Flame separation is an illusion and no matter how far you are separated from your Twin Flame, you feel tethered to each other energetically. Once you Surrender, you realize that the depth of your connection is infinite and you feel the love in your heart grows stronger and purer every day.

Surrendering frees your soul so that you freely feel the love from your Twin Flame without any fear.

Surrender also helps you to find self-love because you know that you deserve to feel as authentic as your Twin Flame inspires you to feel.

The more you allow healing into your life, the more you feel empowered to rediscover your authentic self.

## How do you manage expectations on your Twin Flame journey?

When you are beginning the Twin Flame journey, you have a lot of expectations because you are viewing your experiences from the "normal" romantic relationship style.

You also want to categorize your connection so that you can understand your new feelings because Twin Flame love is magical compared to everyday love.

But, you get disappointed every time you try to control the nature of your Twin Flame relationship because you realize that everything happening to you is divinely guided.

If you have expectations, you start to chase your Twin Flame during the physical separation phase because you want to control the outcomes of your reunion.

The best way to manage the stress of having expectations is by trusting divine timing. There is no phase of your Twin Flame process that is controlled by you.

Your initial encounter was unplanned and unconditional love caught you by surprise. You have no idea as to why you are going through the physical separation phase and you also don't know when it will expire.

When you think of your future, you also know that you have no control over what will happen when you reunite.

Trusting the connection that you feel with your Twin Flame and divine timing are the best ways to manage your expectations. The Twin Flame journey is a personal journey and it is all about you because it is happening within you. Focus on loving yourself and finding your authentic self. Let divine timing take over your journey.

# Inner Balance

It is very blissful once you finally surrender and let your Twin Flame behave the way they do.

You have no control throughout your Twin Flame journey and you cannot alter your process but you can choose to focus on finding inner peace.

Once you accept to let go of the stress of trying to have control, you realize that the Twin Flame journey is all about finding inner peace.

Once you feel grounded in your power, you start to accumulate happiness within yourself which manifests in your physical reality.

I believe that healing is continuous throughout the Twin Flame journey and having inner resistance to change and grow can ground you in constant emotional pain.

You must open your heart to embrace your journey and the more you accept your Twin Flame experience, the easier it becomes to progress further in harmony.

Once you find inner harmony, you do not worry at all because you feel the connection within you every day.

When you are grounded in emotional pain, it is easy to doubt your Twin Flame connection because the emotional chaos clouds your judgment.

# Shared Pain

There is no beginning or end to the Twin Flame connection. It just is what it is.

I always channel my Twin Flame's emotional pain if he is feeling sad or emotionally chaotic. I feel his longing sometimes and it is very difficult to move on because you are constantly pulled into the connection whether you like it or not.

I stopped telling myself that I can easily move on from feeling his energy because I do not have any control over it.

The Twin Flame energy is all about accepting to embrace your shared energy with your Twin Flame because once you acknowledge each other, you are triggered into a spiritual awakening.

The spiritual awakening of Twin Flames triggers you to cleanse your energy. You then start to feel the energetic merge with your Twin Flame.

Once you experience the energetic merge with your Twin Flame, you cease to feel like your old self. You feel different because the shared energy of Oneness with your Twin Flame keeps growing and refining itself.

You start to operate as one single energetic unit with your Twin Flame. Meeting your Twin Flame changes every aspect of your journey starting with how you feel.

Because of the shared energy of oneness that you have with your Twin Flame, you feel their energy whether they are feeling happy or sad.

*Does your Twin Flame feel your sadness and emotions?*

Because of the energetic Oneness that Twin Flames share, you always channel each other's longing and desires.

Because of the Soul intimacy, that you share with your Twin Flame, you sometimes feel like you live in each other's minds.

You as if you are always compelled to chase your Twin Flame because you feel their intense feelings.

When I feel sad, I always feel a distinct energetic feedback loop as if my Twin Flame knows how I feel. Sometimes if I am crying, I feel like his essence is comforting me and hovering all over me.

When he is sad, I always know how he is feeling. I feel excruciating emotional pain coiling around my heart area and it intensifies if I don't acknowledge it.

Sometimes my heart area feels warm with intense energy and sometimes I puke first so that I can have some relief from the intensity of the emotions.

Sometimes I break down and start sobbing.

I have been through the most distinct stages of my Twin Flame journey and whether I am feeling happy or sad, I always think of my Twin Flame.

There is no having a break from thinking about a Twin Flame and the thoughts intensify as you progress further on your journey.

I believe that you keep having constant thoughts of your Twin Flame because of the Soul intimacy that you share. You feel the energetic Oneness in your

Soul and the more you try to block out thoughts of them, the more you crave to remember them.

I met my Twin Flame three years ago and I think of him every minute of the day. I keep remembering his eyes and how happy he makes me feel.

Also, the other reason why I think of my Twin Flame all the time is that I miss the good feelings his presence brings to me.

I miss feeling safe with him because my Twin Flame is my home. My soul feels an emptiness because I miss him. I crave to fill the emptiness in my soul with his presence.

Every day it feels like half of myself is missing because my Twin Flame is absent.

# Dreaming of a Twin Flame

The soul connection between Twin Flames is infinite. You feel your soul growing and expanding as you grow in Oneness.

Once you accept your new situation as a Twin Flame, you accept the shared energy that you share with your Twin Flame. You let the connection consume you and you learn to embrace the oneness with your divine partner.

For me, I always feel the soul connection with my Twin Flame and I wake up feeling happy and energetically rejuvenated.

Sometimes it is the intense energy that wakes me up in the middle of the night and sometimes I feel it the moment I open my eyes in the morning.

My Twin Flame has never left me even though we have been separated for three years because I feel him energetically always.

# Thinking of each other 24/7

If you have been on the Twin Flame journey for a long time, you understand that a Twin Flame Separation is an Illusion because you still feel the connection growing within you every day and your thoughts constantly race towards them.

The Twin Flame Journey surprisingly gets very interesting as it progresses because you know in your soul that your divine partner is one of a kind and special.

Thinking of your Twin Flame starts from the moment you acknowledge each other and it is not constant incessant thinking of your Twin Flame but rather a remembrance of them.

Your soul remembers them, and you keep wondering how you know your Twin Flame from before. It always feels like you shared past lives.

When you are separated from each other even though temporarily, your soul keeps calling you to merge with your Twin Flame and the energetic pulling keeps reminding you of how your Twin Flame makes you feel.

Twin Flame love is like a euphoric drug and if your Twin Flame is gone for too long, you crash like you are going through withdrawal.

The energetic oneness that you share with your Twin Flame takes you over and you feel like you are merging energetically, mentally, and emotionally.

You feel as if you share the same mind with your Twin Flame and you sometimes feel like you can channel their emotions and feelings.

No matter how much you try to block out thoughts of your Twin Flame, you feel like they are you and you are them. You feel the energetic singularity and a Soul Oneness.

As you progress further on your Twin Flame Journey, you begin to understand that once you meet your Twin Flame, everything in your life revolves around you and your Twin Flame Connection.

The Twin Flame encounter brings so much change in your life starting with how you feel.

The Twin Flame journey is about learning to embrace the shared energy of Oneness.

# The EGO

*Do you think that your ego gets in the way of your Twin Flame journey?*

My Twin Flame said to me that I have no ego, but I do. It is because my ego dissolves when I am with him. I feel disarmed when he is present and he breaks down all my ego walls.

On the other hand, his work and profession are centred on having an ego and looking powerful. He said that his work is all about having power.

When he is with me though, his ego dissolves as well. He shows me a side to himself that is vulnerable, defenceless, and childlike.

I always hang out with his inner child because my Twin Flame shows to me the cutest and silliest side to him.

During physical separation though, my Twin Flame has found it very difficult to balance his ego with what he feels.

He says that it is best for everyone if we do not talk but I text him when I feel compelled to and he sometimes responds and suddenly stops as we converse.

I am used to his sudden disappearance; One minute he is chatty, sweet, and cute but then the next minute he just doesn't respond to me or he becomes cold and distant.

I chose to trust how I feel in my heart and my soul because I feel our connection every second of the day whether they are good feelings of euphoria and bliss or sad feelings of longing and desire.

I learned to harness my energy to stay strong within no matter how I feel at a certain moment. I found ways to manage to be happy in my physical life situation even though I miss him.

I learned to balance my Twin Flame situation with creating a happy life for myself because I do not know when he will be back to me.

Life has to go on whether your Twin Flame situation is going great or not. I found a life purpose; something that I can focus my newfound Twin Flame energy.

You need to find something meaningful that impacts other people so that you can channel your Twin Flame love to help others. You do not need to save the world, but you can impact a life in your little corner of the world.

Twin Flame energy is a blessing and not everyone has the privilege to feel the bliss and inner harmony that the Twin Flame connection brings to you once you learn to embrace the shared energy of Oneness.

Once you feel the energetic harmony with your Twin Flame, you learn to harness your shared energy to improve your life. You feel effortless in everything that you do because you are two in one.

Your Twin Flame never leaves you energetically no matter how far they drift from you physically.

I have learned that the Twin Flame experience is very difficult and challenging at first but it gets easier and better the more you learn to embrace the new energy.

You must accept yourself to change because inner resistance only brings to you frustration and pain. Soon or later, you have to change because the Twin Flame experience only stands to change you and your life situation.

Change is very difficult to embrace but you eventually learn to go with the flow. It starts with accepting yourself and who you are from within.

This is the first challenge of the Twin Flame experience because you go deep within yourself to dig out all the past pain and core wounding. You must acknowledge every broken part of you and you are tasked to love parts of yourself that you thought were unlovable.

Unconditional love for your Twin Flame inspires you to grow the inner strength to accept and acknowledge yourself. This is why your Twin Flame is your mirror because they love you unconditionally and you are inspired to do the same for yourself.

If you are not used to feeling love for yourself, you are challenged to submit to self-love. Self-love is authentic and very difficult to embrace.

You cannot love someone else if you do not know how to love yourself. You cannot appreciate love if you do not know what it is.

The Twin Flame separation phase is a blessing in disguise because it challenges you to face yourself.

Remember that you are always craving to feel your Twin Flame love and you always want to be close to them. The compulsion to be in the vicinity of your Twin Flame is a natural desire. This is why you are constantly thinking of your Twin Flame every day after your first encounter.

During the physical separation phase, you are challenged to first embrace the unconditional love for yourself before you show it to your Twin Flame. You are challenged to feel love for yourself first before you try to express it to your Twin Flame.

This is a very emotionally challenging situation because you first experience the confusion and frustration that change brings to you.

You know deep down in your soul that for you to become the authentic version of yourself, you must first change the different aspects of yourself and your life.

There is no shortcut to the Twin Flame journey because your Soul is constantly calling you to change so that you can embrace the newfound Twin Flame energy.

If you resist the change that needs to be done in your life, you feel restless and helpless daily because you can not hide from how you feel within.

Even though you try to go into a new relationship with someone else so that you can distract yourself, you are constantly craving to check in on your Twin Flame because it is a natural compulsion.

Even though you distance yourself from your Twin Flame in the physical, you cannot switch off thoughts of them because your Soul keeps reminding you of the Oneness that you feel.

You will eventually submit to the Twin Flame connection no matter how long it takes to acknowledge and accept how you feel.

*On the twin flame journey, is it possible that the awakened twin is the first to run instead of chasing? I'm a Divine Feminine that is awake to the connection but I'm running from my Twin Flame.*

From my experiences, I was both the runner and the chaser — I was the one who first ran from the connection because I was overwhelmed, and once I realized that the connection that I have with him is special, I started to chase him back by apologizing for trying to block him out of my life.

I believe that once you start to learn about the Twin Flame experiences, you realize that there is no distinction between the runner and the chaser. You both experience the energetic turbulence in your connection that affects the running and chasing process.

I also believe that if you are doing more energetic clearing, you are the one driving the energetic flow of the connection. If you are more centered in your energy, then you are most likely to be responsible for grounding your Twin Flame.

You are also responsible for ending the running and chasing cycle; Once you realize the dynamics and workings of the running and chasing, you can influence how your Twin Flame responds to your actions.

If you have been the chaser, you can choose to surrender, and if you are running from the connection, you can choose to face your journey and embrace your fears.

I believe that knowing about the workings of the Twin Flame experience is an added advantage to being on the Twin Flame journey.

*Does it bother you when your Twin Flame does not Wish you a Happy Birthday?*

Due to the estranged communication between you and your Twin Flame, you will end up not communicating at all especially when you believe that it matters when they wish you a happy birthday or send you season's greetings during the festive holidays.

It is more infuriating when you see your Twin Flame online sometimes and responding to other people on social media but even though you reach out, they tend to ignore you.

From my experience being on this Twin Flame journey for almost three years, I now understand that it is not personal when your Twin Flame does not reach out especially if they are resisting the feelings they have for you.

One day when they give you an explanation for their behavior, it will eventually make sense to you why they were ignoring you. Sometimes it is for the best to give your Twin Flame space to let them work through their Twin Flame situation.

Twin Flame love is very overwhelming and it catches you by surprise and if your Twin Flame is overwhelmed by how they feel, it is a natural response to the intense unconditional love that grows every day within them.

You always feel the Twin Flame love growing within you. You eventually understand that you d not need to be physical with your Twin Flame to feel the connection.

I tried wishing my Twin Flame a happy birthday twice but he kept ignoring me, and he never wished me a happy birthday directly but he would check in with our mutual friends to find out if I was having a good time.

Your Twin Flame loves you very much believe it or not.

*During the Twin Flame Journey, who changes drastically? The runner or the chaser?*

Change in Twin Flames is Alchemical. There is no degree to which you can measure it or influence it. The Soul Cleanse process will transform the two individuals who are involved in the Twin Flame Journey until they are both transformed into their Authentic beings.

If you look at it from the energetic point of view, both Twin Flames share the same core signature vibration. This means that there is no distinction between the two energies of the divine partners; (chaser or runner).

As the Twin Flames grow into their Twin Flame energy by learning to balance it within themselves, the two individuals strengthen their core shared Twin Flame energy.

When you quiet yourself from within and listen to your soul, you will feel your Twin Flame feel you back. You just know in your gut how they are feeling for you by feeling the energy within yourself because your Twin Flame is you.

Yes, physical change can happen and sometimes it seems drastic but I challenge you to look at this from an energetic perspective not from a physical separation point of view because Twin Flames are each other.

*What is the Twin Flame Chaser Pain and how do you overcome it?*

The compulsion to chase your Twin Flame is intensified during the physical separation phase because of the Soul intimacy that you share.

The obsessive behavior to always constantly check in with your Twin Flame is a trigger to push you to go deep within yourself to understand every part of your soul.

Chasing a Twin Flame is a temporary phase because you eventually face yourself and you cleanse your past pain and heal your core wounding that exists within you.

Don't feel guilty for chasing your Twin Flame because it is only a phase and it passes quickly once you submit to self-love and inner healing.

The time comes when you find inner peace and you surrender to your connection.

Your Twin Flame will come back to you eventually when they feel ready to confront the situation because you cannot escape unconditional love no matter how far you run from each other.

A Twin Flame reunion is imminent and no obstacle is big enough to get in the way of Twin Flames.

*How do you let go of chasing your Twin Flame Runner and focus on yourself?*

This seems challenging at first especially if you are still new to how the Twin Flame dynamic works and it gets more complicated when you want to Surrender but you are still compelled to constantly check in on your Twin Flame.

I tried blocking him out of my life but it did not work. I blocked his social media but I wanted to unblock him and he refused to add me back after I sabotaged our friendship. I tried to delete his contact information but sometimes he would bounce back in my life with a simple message and it would trigger me back to chasing him.

I tried to block the connection by focusing on dating other people but the more I resisted feeling the connection, there was an increase in the signs reminding me of him like his birthday digits popping up on my screen, and sometimes I ended up dating guys who resembled him which made me miss the effortless sacred bond that I share with my Twin Flame.

I learned that there is no running or hiding from a Twin Flame connection. You must ACCEPT your new Twin Flame situation and learn to work with it to create more peace and harmony within yourself which also affects your shared energy with your Twin Flame.

# Running into relationships

I also did that. I tried to find suitors. I don't know your reasons and I won't speculate but for me, I felt like the Universe was blocking me.

I felt trapped every time I tried to find someone. I knew deep within that I was running from myself and trying to hide behind other relationships and people only left me feeling isolated and lonely.

It felt like purgatory; there was no specific map to help me come out of my misery.

Only you know the truth of how you feel within.

If you genuinely want to move on and date someone new, the Universe would let you.

I believe that the Universe is sending you signs that your journey is not yet over.

You both suffer endless heartaches in quiet desperation. You live in purgatory forever until you confront the situation. The true Twin Flame nature is Union. You are already one — you have to break from the chains of the Human condition to realize wholeness.

*What do you do if your Twin Flame is married?*

It is excruciating meeting your Twin Flame but when they are married. It is complicated if your Twin Flame is married with children.

You do not choose the Twin Flame encounter and you also do not choose your Twin Flame.

Twin Flames meet in the rarest of situations and you cannot control the triggers even though you are not physically together.

Once the encounter happens and you recognize each other, change takes over both your lives.

There is no greater love than a Twin Flame connection and once you find each other, you realize that all you desire is to merge in every way possible.

Even though your Twin Flame is married, they can go through emotional and spiritual changes and they miss you as much as you miss them.

You feel the oneness with your Twin Flame and you are always compelled to change your life so that you can be together.

Change between Twin Flames is inevitable and you know it within you that as long as you both walk the earth, you will never be happy with anyone else if you are not together.

# Reunion

I always have the end in mind — it is easy to feel stuck in the separation cycle. I realized that if you and your Twin Flame discuss the plans for the future, you focus on that.

Having goals gives you a sense of purpose and it also sets a structure for your days. It also boosts your sense of wellbeing.

You feel dedicated to aspiring to a reunion. Focusing on your goals also moves you from feeling stuck to progressing every day. You focus on tracking your progress.

You also have a paradigm shift — you feel hopeful. You have a sense of purpose. When you channel the love that you feel for your Twin Flame into something meaningful that uplifts others. It heals you.

The runner Twin Flame will eventually return when you are ready.

I haven't seen mine either in 3 years but I feel him with me all the time.

Yesterday was the worst:

I had a lovely day — I felt happy because I felt him in my dreams.

I meditated and sent love to him in my heart for over an hour.

After a couple of hours, I was hit by an intense wave of sad feelings. I knew right away that it was him.

My heart sunk — I went into an emotional funk. A part of my body felt his pain.

My knees felt weak — I suddenly broke down into tears and sobbed for over 30 minutes until the sad feelings dissipated. After I cried out the pain, I felt better.

*How do you let a Twin Flame go?*

This trick worked for me yesterday. I felt his pain and cried like a baby. , Afterward, I said positive words to myself like; I accept my feelings. I accept feeling unconditional love. I love my beloved. I feel you. I love you.

Every time I gave love to myself, I felt the tension calm down. I suddenly felt him sending love back to me. I smiled.

You have to accept your new life situation after the encounter and go with the flow of the course of the Twin Flame process. Surrender begins with acceptance as you gradually free yourself from controlling your Twin Flame relationship.

Surrender cannot be faked -- you eventually let go when you are ready to forgive yourself and your Twin Flame. Forgiveness frees you from your fears.

For me, I found forgiveness when I told my Twin Flame the truth of my heart. I knew that even though we were estranged, at least he knew where I stood with our situation. After that, I focused on bringing happiness back into my life.

The more I focused on loving myself, it felt like I was loving my Twin Flame more. I then learned that we are not separated after all. A reunion with a Twin Flame or a physical relationship is only icing on the cake. You are the CAKE!

*Take whatever memories, and experiences you created with your Twin Flame and build a life of blessings, success, and abundance. Embrace the unconditional love connection that you feel to your beloved to heal yourself and your life situation.*

*When the stars re-align again just like your initial encounter, you will reunite. Make sure that you are ready spiritually, mentally, emotionally, and energetically. You were meant to find each other in this lifetime.*

*Do not shortchange yourself. You carry unconditional love within — give some to yourself!*

No matter what you try, you cannot control your Twin Flame's response.

It is difficult I know; you gotta keep moving forward.

For me, I channeled the love I have for him into something meaningful— I did everything in his memory. I put the Twin Flame energy into serving others.

The more I feel good about myself and what I do, the more I feel closer to my Twin Flame.

Sometimes I look at myself in the mirror and smile — I say to myself; "If only he could see me now!"

My Twin Flame can date and also marry whoever he wants — he is free but I know that we are already married in spirit and Soul. I also know that I am one of a kind to him.

Lately, I treat myself as a Spiritual being going through a Human Condition.

I am so grateful for the blessings and gifts of being a Twin Flame.

Well, from my understanding and experience, Chasing or Running behaviors are only terminologies to grasp the Twin Flame energetic dance.

Before a physical union occurs, you have to first attain inner union.

It does not matter who is chasing or running — you are your Twin Flame.

Because of the mirror effect, you reflect on each other your deepest desires and greatest fears.

Even though you both want to have a physical marriage, you will not enjoy it if either of you is hurting within.

On top of this, you feel each other's grief — my Twin Flame's pain hurts me more than mine. This is because I have no control over how intense it gets; I can only let it pass through me.

I have been both the runner and chaser you understand that there is no distinction between the two terminologies.

You don't feel any separation within because your energy keeps merging into oneness with your Spiritual lover.

On top of this, even though you choose to deny the connection and also hide from your Twin Flame, you go through Spiritual growth — your Twin Flame's energetic work boosts your healing and accelerates the Spiritual Awakening process.

You eventually feel the energetic oneness. You live inside your Twin Flame.

# Runner Returns

When you feel that the connection with a Twin Flame is real, you go through different stages of accepting all the emotions. This is why I advise fellow Twin Flames who are runners to accept the nature of the connection no matter how uncomfortable the feelings are.

I have learned that the Twin Flame connection is all about finding the balance between holding and letting go. Once you are triggered into the awakening, there is no turning back to how you used to know life. You must adapt to the flow and keep moving forward.

Once you let yourself feel the uncomfortable feelings that a Twin Flame triggers within you -- accept your new reality.

The reason why you deny the connection is because you know within you that it is real. You sometimes feel cursed because you cannot control how you feel.

At some point, you will have to confront the situation and your Twin Flame. You will have to look into their eyes again -- you will still feel triggered into chasing or running if you are not yet healed.

The truth is that if your Twin Flame is real, he or she will return — this is a very uncomfortable reality to accept.

For me, I sometimes feel ready to see him but then when I analyze my situation more, I still see so many changes that I have to make even though I do my best every day to prepare for the reunion.

I feel nervous when I think of moving continents; I know that it is going to happen. I feel anxious when I think of restarting my life again with him. I worry about the uncertainty of the future.

I just have to give it a shot I guess.

# Signs of inner union

- You feel unceasing inner harmony; you sit in your power. You feel unhurried — you are in control of your feelings. You feel endless inner peace. You feel connected to the source of your being.

- You do not worry about your Twin Flame's behavior. You feel the connection within you. You know for sure that he or she feels the same way. After you feel complete union within, you feel eternally married to your Twin Flame. You relax and watch your life unfold as it was divinely planned.

- You feel no envy or jealousy in case your Twin Flame is dating someone else. You have no fear that the connection would fade. You instead pity whoever your Twin Flame is dating because you know that you have an eternal pact with him or her. You also understand that even though your Twin Flame chooses to move on and marry someone else, you have their Soul. You know for sure that as long as you both walk the earth, you will never be happy with anyone else but each other.

- You trust the divine to guide your journey. If you were trying to be the driver of your Twin Flame bus, you give up the keys to the Universe and trust that you will arrive at your destination happily.

*Is the Twin Flame Union all about you?*

Yes, indeed! The Twin Flame Union is a process of realizing that you have shared energy with your Twin Flame.

I call the shared energy that I feel with my Twin Flame the energy of Oneness.

If you have not yet learned to embrace the shared energy with your Twin Flame, you feel emotional turbulence.

The chaotic emotions that you feel are a sign that you haven't yet unified yourself within and this situation happens when you resist the connection within.

This is why usually there is a temporary physical separation between Twin Flames to understand what is happening to them and why they feel the complicated emotions.

The complicated emotions rise to the surface because of the energetic merge.

Before you learn to balance your energy from within, you always feel like your Twin Flame's energy is constantly merging with yours.

You feel their essence hover all over you and you are always channeling their feelings and emotions.

Once you accept that you will always feel connected to your Twin Flame, you gradually start accepting the new shared energy of Oneness.

Before Oneness happens, you go through a phase of energy cleansing so that you can merge with your Twin Flame harmoniously.

Once you embrace the energetic share with your Twin Flame, it changes you completely because you go through an alchemical change so that you are your authentic self.

When you start vibrating at a frequency of energetic Oneness with your Twin Flame, your life magically changes because the shared energy with your Twin Flame brings you inner peace, harmony, and bliss.

You eventually learn to balance your energy and when you do, you start to discover the magic of being a Twin Flame.

When you feel unified within with the Oneness with
your Twin Flame, it is what Twin Flame Union is
called.

This is why Twin Flame Separation is an illusion.

The Soul does not know separation because it does
not acknowledge the physical distance between
you and your Twin Flame.

The Twin Flame journey is about unifying yourself
from within and allowing yourself to change into
your authentic self so that you can embrace the
newfound emery of Twin Flame Oneness.

# About the Author

After having experienced the Twin Flame Journey for over three years, Silvia Moon is committed to inspiring other Twin Flames.  She uses her self-help books as a platform to share her insights.

She is determined to use her experiences to support fellow Twin Flames by sharing simple, practical, and inspirational self-help advice.

She also shares stories from her previous experiences as a Twin Flame newbie. She understands your frustration if you are new to the Twin Flame process; everything seems complicated and confusing.

If you are a Twin Flame going through the challenging separation phase, Silvia is here to inspire you to aspire to a harmonious reunion.
Silvia is hoping to inspire you to keep believing in your Twin Flame connection. She is also excited to act as a facilitator to guiding any Twin Flame who is new to the confusing Twin Flame journey.

After having gone through the stressful chasing and running phases of the Twin Flame process, Silvia found healing and inner peace. She learned that the Twin Flame journey is a Battle Within The Self.

She is hoping to be your guide as you compare and contrast your experiences with hers.  Silvia understands your pain, frustration, and confusion if you are new to the Twin Flame experience because she has been where you are.

She shares her experiences to help you have a fresh perspective. She hopes to inspire you to enjoy your Twin Flame process if you feel stuck on your journey.

Do not miss out on the self-help tips she shares throughout her books. She indicates practical changes that you can make to transform your life.

Stay Blessed!